THE US CONSTITUTION

BY BRAY JACOBSON

Gareth Stevens
PUBLISHING

CRASHCOURSE

Please visit our website, www.garethstevens.com. For a free color catalog of all our high-quality books, call toll free 1-800-542-2595 or fax 1-877-542-2596.

Library of Congress Cataloging-in-Publication Data

Names: Jacobson, Bray, author.
Title: The US Constitution / Bray Jacobson.
Description: New York : Gareth Stevens Publishing, [2018] | Series: A look at US history | Includes index.
Identifiers: LCCN 2016040680| ISBN 9781482460438 (pbk. book) | ISBN 9781482460445 (6 pack) | ISBN 9781482460452 (library bound book)
Subjects: LCSH: United States. Constitution--Juvenile literature. | Constitutional history--United States--Juvenile literature.
Classification: LCC E303 .J25 2018 | DDC 342.7302/9--dc23
LC record available at https://lccn.loc.gov/2016040680

First Edition

Published in 2018 by
Gareth Stevens Publishing
111 East 14th Street, Suite 349
New York, NY 10003

Copyright © 2018 Gareth Stevens Publishing

Designer: Samantha DeMartin
Editor: Kristen Nelson

Photo credits: Series art Christophe BOISSON/Shutterstock.com; (feather quill) Galushko Sergey/Shutterstock.com; (parchment) mollicart-design/Shutterstock.com; cover, pp. 1, 17 GraphicaArtis/Archive Photos/Getty Images; p. 5 MPI/ArchivePhotos/Getty Images; p. 7 Hulton Archive/Archive Photos/Getty Images; pp. 9, 15 (Hamilton) Everett - Art/Shutterstock.com; p. 13 Universal History Archive/Universal Images Group/Getty Images; pp. 15 (Morris), 23 Everett Historical/Shutterstock.com; p. 21 FPG/Getty Images; p. 27 Scewing/Wikimedia Commons; p. 29 Allen Russell/Getty Images.

Printed in the United States of America

CPSIA compliance information: Batch #CS17GS: For further information contact Gareth Stevens, New York, New York at 1-800-542-2595.

CONTENTS

Words in the glossary appear in **bold** type the first time they are used in the text.

THE FOUNDATION OF A NATION

The US Constitution is the highest law in the United States. It created the US government, dividing the power into three branches so no one part would be too powerful. Today, it's still the **foundation** of how the country is run.

ARTICLES

OF

Confederation

AND

Perpetual Union

BETWEEN THE *J.H.M*

STATES

OF

NEW-HAMPSHIRE, MASSACHUSETTS-BAY, RHODE-ISLAND AND PROVIDENCE PLANTATIONS, CONNECTICUT, NEW-YORK, NEW-JERSEY, PENNSYLVANIA, DELAWARE, MARYLAND, VIRGINIA, NORTH-CAROLINA, SOUTH-CAROLINA AND GEORGIA.

MAKE THE GRADE

The first constitution was called the Articles of Confederation. The **document** gave US states a lot of independence, but the central government was too weak.

LANCASTER:

PRINTED BY FRANCIS BAILEY.

M,DCC,LXXVII.

A NEW DOCUMENT

In May 1787, **delegates** from 12 states met in Philadelphia, Pennsylvania. The Constitutional **Convention** started as a meeting to make the Articles of Confederation better. Early on, the delegates realized they needed to write a whole new document!

MAKE THE GRADE

Many of the Founding Fathers were at the convention, including Benjamin Franklin and George Washington, who was named the president of the Constitutional Convention.

MAKING COMPROMISES

The delegates didn't agree on some subjects, and the US Constitution is the result of many **compromises**. One of the first was how states would be **represented** in Congress. The Virginia Plan said representation should be based on population. This favored states with many people.

James Madison, author of the Virginia Plan

MAKE THE GRADE

The New Jersey Plan said all states should have the same number of representatives. This would allow states with smaller populations to have an equal say in government.

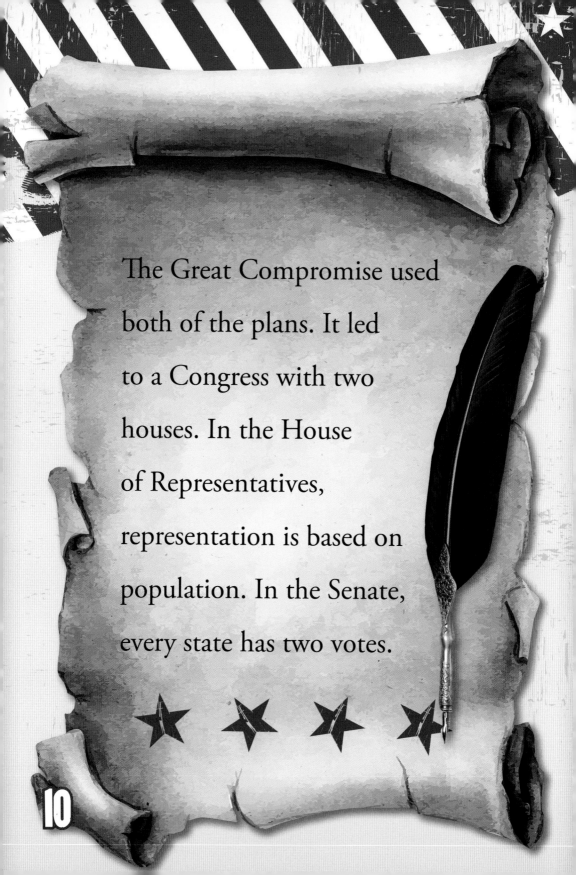

The Great Compromise used both of the plans. It led to a Congress with two houses. In the House of Representatives, representation is based on population. In the Senate, every state has two votes.

Three Branches of the US Government

LEGISLATIVE BRANCH	EXECUTIVE BRANCH	JUDICIAL BRANCH
MAKES LAWS	CARRIES OUT LAWS	EXPLAINS AND RULES ON LAWS
HEADED BY CONGRESS	HEADED BY THE PRESIDENT	HEADED BY THE SUPREME COURT

MAKE THE GRADE

Congress is the legislative, or lawmaking, branch of government. The US Constitution also created the judicial and executive branches.

When considering representation, the delegates had to agree on how slaves would be counted toward a state's population. At the time, about one-fifth of the population was slaves. The Three-Fifths Compromise said that for every five slaves, three would be counted.

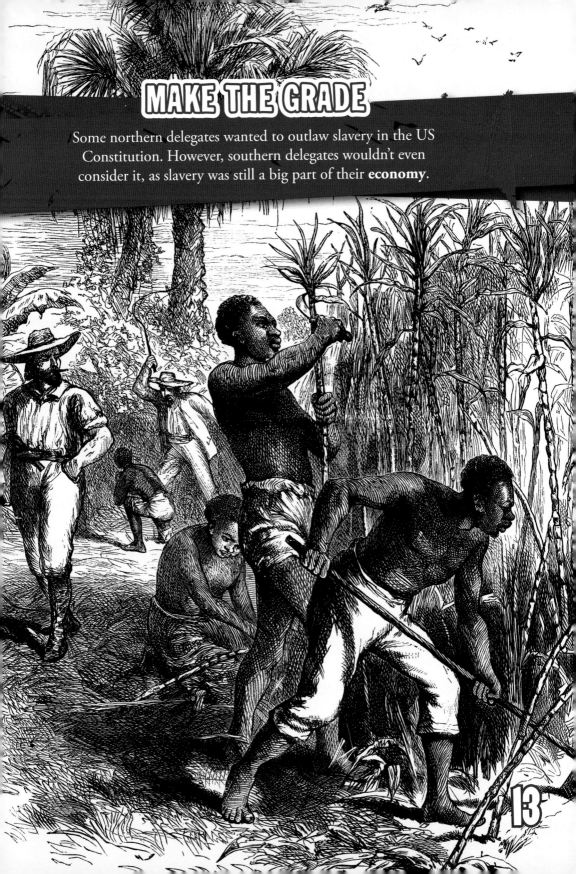

MAKE THE GRADE

Some northern delegates wanted to outlaw slavery in the US Constitution. However, southern delegates wouldn't even consider it, as slavery was still a big part of their **economy**.

13

PRESENTING THE US CONSTITUTION

The first **draft** of the US Constitution was finished on August 6, 1787. After the delegates **debated** it for about a month, five men were chosen to rewrite it. They presented the finished document on September 12.

Alexander
Hamilton

Gouverneur
Morris

MAKE THE GRADE

Alexander Hamilton of New York, William Samuel Johnson of
Connecticut, Gouverneur Morris of Pennsylvania, James Madison
of Virginia, and Rufus King of Massachusetts were chosen to write
the final draft of the US Constitution.

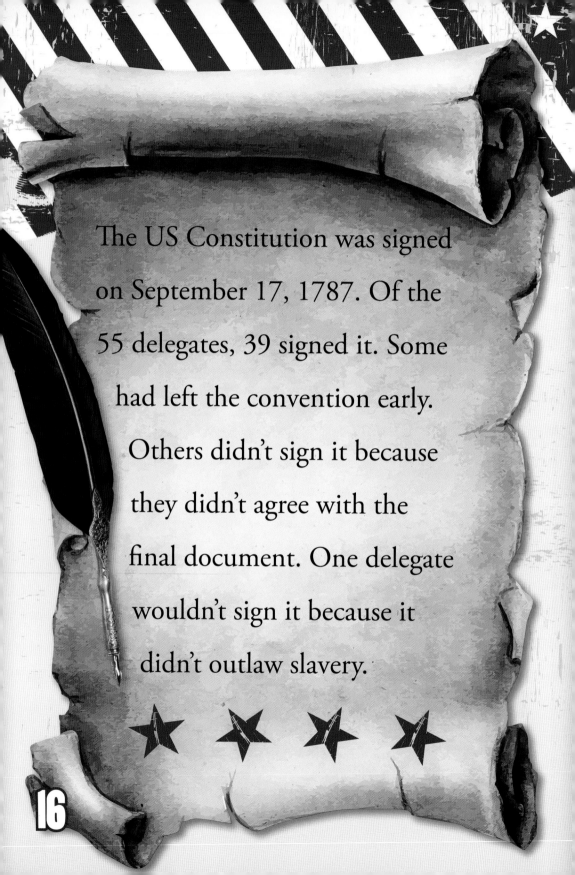

The US Constitution was signed on September 17, 1787. Of the 55 delegates, 39 signed it. Some had left the convention early. Others didn't sign it because they didn't agree with the final document. One delegate wouldn't sign it because it didn't outlaw slavery.

The US Constitution is the oldest written national constitution still in use!

WHAT DOES IT SAY?

There are seven articles, or parts, of the US Constitution. Article I forms Congress and gives it lawmaking powers and other duties. It states who can serve in the House of Representatives and the Senate and for how long.

Who Can Serve in Congress?

	HOUSE OF REPRESENTATIVES	SENATE
AGE	must be 25 or older	must be 30 or older
LENGTH OF CITIZENSHIP	at least 7 years	at least 9 years
LENGTH OF TERM	2 years	6 years

MAKE THE GRADE

The preamble, or introduction, of the US Constitution states that the people of the United States are setting up laws for their nation, including those for keeping peace, **protection**, and making sure **citizens** live happily and freely.

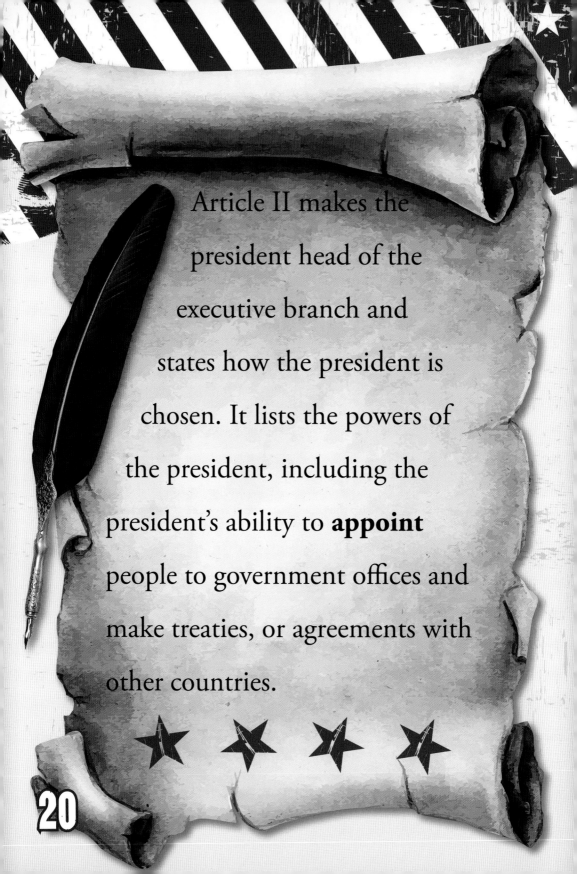

Article II makes the president head of the executive branch and states how the president is chosen. It lists the powers of the president, including the president's ability to **appoint** people to government offices and make treaties, or agreements with other countries.

MAKE THE GRADE

The US Constitution gives the president veto power, or the ability to stop a bill in Congress from becoming law.

The third article sets up the Supreme Court, the highest court in the United States. The article allows Congress to make laws about who can become a justice, or one who sits on the court, as well as how many justices there will be.

The Supreme Court mainly hears cases having to do with the Constitution. It tries to make the Constitution's meaning clear and useful for today's problems.

The US Supreme Court, around 1915

The fourth article of the US Constitution allows for the addition of more states in the future and says how that should happen. In the fifth article, the two ways the document can be amended, or changed, are laid out.

Amending the Constitution

⭐ **An amendment is introduced.** ➡️ **Two-thirds of the House and Senate pass the amendment.** ➡️ **Three-fourths of states pass the amendment.**

⭐ **Two-thirds of states call for a constitutional convention.** ➡️ **Amendments are introduced during the convention.** ➡️ **Three-fourths of states pass the amendments.**

MAKE THE GRADE

Since its writing, the US Constitution has been amended 27 times. Only the first way shown above has been used to do so.

RATIFICATION

In order for the Constitution to become the law of the land, nine of the 13 states had to ratify, or agree to, it. Delaware was the first to ratify it on December 7, 1787. The Constitution finally went into effect on March 9, 1789.

JOHN JAY
wrote five of the 85 articles of the Federalist Papers

MAKE THE GRADE

A group in favor of the Constitution called themselves the Federalists. They wrote a series of articles called the Federalist Papers trying to get states to vote for ratification.

ADDING CIVIL RIGHTS

The first Congress of the new nation met in 1789. Soon after, they passed 10 amendments to the Constitution promising citizens certain civil rights. Civil rights are the personal freedoms granted to US citizens by law. These amendments are called the Bill of Rights.

MAKE THE GRADE

Some of the civil rights included in the Bill of Rights are freedom of speech, the right to a fair trial, the right to peaceful assembly, and more.

29

TIMELINE OF THE US CONSTITUTION

March 1, 1781

The Articles of Confederation passes.

May 25, 1787

The Constitutional Convention begins.

September 17, 1787

The US Constitution is signed.

June 21, 1788

New Hampshire becomes the ninth state to ratify the Constitution.

March 4, 1789

The US Constitution goes into effect.

September 25, 1789

Congress passes the Bill of Rights.

GLOSSARY

appoint: to choose for a position

citizen: someone who lives in a country legally and has certain rights

compromise: a way of two sides reaching agreement in which each gives up something to end an argument

convention: a gathering of people who have a common interest or purpose

debate: to argue a side

delegate: a representative to a convention

document: a formal piece of writing

draft: the first try at a piece of writing

economy: the money made in an area and how it is spent

foundation: the base on which something stands

protection: the act of keeping something safe

represent: to serve by being given the authority, or power, to do so

FOR MORE INFORMATION

Books

Baxter, Roberta. *The Creation of the US Constitution: A History Perspectives Book*. Ann Arbor, MI: Cherry Lake Publishing, 2015.

Wolfe, James, and Heather Moehn. *Understanding the US Constitution*. New York, NY: Enslow Publishing, 2016.

Websites

Constitution of the United States: A Transcription
archives.gov/exhibits/charters/constitution_transcript.html
You can read what the US Constitution actually says here!

INDEX